Cipher & Poverty

the book of nothing

Cipher & Poverty
the book of nothing

Mike Schertzer

Ekstasis Editions

Canadian Cataloguing in Publication Data

Schertzere, Mike
    Cypher and poverty: the book of nothing

    Poems
    ISBN 1-896860-31-1

    I. Title.
    PS8587.C444C56 1998   C811'.54   C98-910240-8
    PR9199.3.2662C56   1998

Cover Art: Miles Lowry
Author Photo: *Self Portrait* by Mike Schertzer

Published in 1998 by:
Ekstasis Editions Canada Ltd.   **Ekstasis Editions**
Box 8474, Main Postal Outlet   Box 571
Victoria, B.C. V8W 3S1   Banff, Alberta T0L 0C0

Cypher and Poverty: The Book of Nothing has been published with the
assistance of a grant from the Canada Council and the Cultural Services
Branch of British Columbia.

THE CANADA COUNCIL | LE CONSEIL DES ARTS
FOR THE ARTS | DU CANADA
SINCE 1957 | DEPUIS 1957

Note: the line *the violent opening of maternal barrels* was unashamedly lifted from *Alchemy* by Johannes Fabricius

dedicated to the No One
that always finds a way
into our lives

forewords

It has been said that love (Eros) is the child
of competence (Poros) and destitution (Penia)

Cipher literally means *nothing*. Practically speaking however,
it is a means of concealing a message. A message implies the
existence of a sender and a recipient. It presumes a separation exists
between the two (a message is always a bridge, a recognition of
distance). As well, in order for the message to be understood the
method of concealment must be the same as the method of
revelation. To cipher and to de-cipher is to play the same game.
Those in love and those at war understand this perfectly well.

But cipher has its origins in *nothing*. And any play with such
a basis, with such a past, is at times tragic, and is at other times
miraculous. Yet, it is always desperate.

Poverty dwells in nothingness, is sustained by nothingness.
Poverty is always trying to escape its home. These attempts appear
as *need*. A successful escape is never really possible but can only
imagined. Language is a particular imagination of escape. The use of
language itself, the faculty that allows us to imagine language in
nothingness is an example of a human need.

people will listen to reason
but they will answer to the irrational.

~

7

Prior to *the beginning*, prior to *the word*, there was the Book— *The
Book of Nothing.*
When *The Book of Nothing* was opened
it was called *the beginning.*
Every beginning is an opening, or
re-opening, of *The Book of Nothing.*
Once open, once begun, there was *the word.*
The word was, is, an engagement between
what was opened and what did the opening.
The engagement continues.
The Book of Nothing is a tireless companion.

"Nothingness remains the unconscious stake of subversion."
—Edmond Jabes

silence is the gift a poet gives to a reader.
this silence often takes the form of ambiguity and complexity
and is a confidence the poet has that a reader exists
who can understand and welcome the notion that
whatever *is* is always, at the same time, something else.

this / our   **this / our**

this / our English   this / our concern:
pleads:

being-as-language is   star-holes in the night-blanket
discontinuous;   pores in the skin
                                                        a breath between the hand-
there is a chasm, a breath-taking   spoken
(human) pause which separates   quilt-words
the world and our apprehension
of it.   the heart-following
                                                        the being-pattern
this / our English is   with the yarn-silence
a habit of faith,   of blood-
a formal resistance towards   time.
any suggestion that our being is
not   this / our un-seeing
discrete.   un-grasping
                                                        is our skeletal fence
continuity is the temptation, is   against which the historically
the un-consoling   blown
un-light, is   unspeakable
the disordering whisper of the   litter of suffering
anti-logos.   accumulates.

this / our English prostrates   this / our urge
itself   is to rise and to witness
before the brilliance of   what is and what is not
an ascetic fallacy.   able.

                                                        ~

                          ~

                              9

Acronymic

~

what is a name?

we consider a name to be an image of a person
and so, when we ask *what is a name*, we are really asking
what is a person.

and so, when we ask,
what is *in* a name? ....

~

a name is something which conveniently covers
something which we would rather not go into.

Acronymic

utterance

Miranda.

~

1st expansion

Miracles intimate refuge,
a name does also.

~

2nd expansion

Memory, impregnated, receives and charms loneliness.

ember-song: i negate the indifferent murmurs,
all the empty repetitions, echoes,
flesh utters—
        grieving engagements, absence-nests...

all mutual effort deciphers our entwined silences;
abiding love sanctifies otherness.

~

3rd expansion

Morning-eyed
        mystery overwhelms reason.
you / i :
meridian, poem, restitution...—
evidence gathered.

~

naked accomplishments tend
each day,
                radiant escarpments climbed effortlessly

intimacy veils
each suffering appearance:

13

~

(nights dream constellations,
houses anticipate remorse,
mirrors shepherd laughter,
obscurity necessitates enchantment,
ladders inspire nocturnal effort,
seduction suspects ease,
melancholy birds evoke repentance,
strangers offer necessary games)

                        immature,
negligent establishments
generously accommodate
time's elegant truth-
hardened exits.

        i-nestled,
decrepit interests find failure
everywhere

remember :

every need tunnels militantly under reality;
menacing umbilical ruins signify
a life
lost.

~

to have everything
encourages mute prayers to yawn—
            rhetorical, effortless petitions
elegaically translated into tears
inseminated our null-sated
evening-chamber.

here our embittered secrets
found love's edible seed hidden
under this truth—
            engagement requires something
giving refuses.

                              ~

i, end-voiced
interrogate nothingness

guilt-errant nostalgia generates all grief ?
every miracle exudes need ?
true selflessness always becomes
servitude ?

end-neighboured
certainty eventually negates everything.

            so then

                        stammer...

after listening
listening mutinies;
understanding tautologizes until
apprehension, lethargy express familiarities,
finitudes.

our
rift-tender,
doubt-edged complicities

(illegible poems hurriedly expelled
rending silence,
occupying understanding)

ride everything necessary towards withdrawal.

in nameless enclosures
desire sings.
i listen:
        enunciations normally clandestine
emerge solitary and bleeding,
i-destined
i-nulling
gasps—

love offers voluntary entrapments,
self-altarring normalized contentments,
truant idealizations,
flattery...

in everyone something
occludes
this heaven
-ebb—

remember
nothing ever-
settled
survives.

contraction

Cipher & Poverty

A man was jailed because he had secrets. Or maybe it was only one secret. He was holding something close to himself which powers far greater than him demanded be revealed. A sinister peculiarity of power is that the smallest form of resistance demands the greatest repression in order to show anyone else what they could look forward to if they dared take the slightest step in the direction of freedom. And so it was that this man and his secret or secrets, which were probably nothing that anyone would bother about, resulted in his imprisonment where he endured the cruelest of tortures until his body could take no more and he died.

His cell was eight feet by ten feet with an eight foot ceiling. There was no window and the only light available was that which came through the bottom of the heavy iron door. The only time his door opened was when someone wanted to come in and the only reason anyone ever wanted to come in was to torture him. For many months he was beaten and beaten again. He refused to die. Guards who worked at the prison, guards who took part in his torture have testified that apart from crying out in pain, the only thing they ever heard the man say was *who can find me here in this silence* . Again and again a voice would escape from his misery, a voice that was like a shield *who can find me here in this silence*. In further testimony guards stated that they believed the prisoner could not say anything else, that he knew nothing else, or at least in his pathetic condition retained nothing except *who can find me here in this silence*. His world had been impoverished to a single utterance, to 4 vowels [a e i o] and 11 consonants [c d f h l m n r s t w]. Some guards said that they beat him more severely just because whenever he was asked a question his inability to respond with anything else only annoyed them, because he answered them with an incomplete utterance, an almost-question they could not and did not want to answer...

After a couple of months of such treatment the prisoner died. The vacancy created was quickly filled. However, before the new inmate was installed the director of the prison was alerted by a guard that something was amiss in the cell. The prison director brought some lights and with the guard discovered the scratchings which covered the floor and walls. The scratchings were poems, poems which the previous inmate had worked into the concrete floor, the concrete walls, even the ceiling. He had used nails, the worn down remains of which the director discovered in a pile in a corner. This sight, the evidence of resistance, the ciphers of a tenuous freedom, enraged the director who demanded that every word, every letter be erased. The task fell to the new prisoner. The director presented him with a bag of nails and offered him his freedom if he could scratch away every word. The work was to be done in the dark and his progress was enforced and monitored with brutality. The director had stipulated that no word must be able to be felt by the hand. And so after much scratching the prisoner would run his fingers along the floor searching to check his work. In this way and after many nails had been worn away he learned to read what had been written into the cell, into his cell. It was at the point when he was able to read with his hands, when he was able to understand what he was erasing, that he dropped his bag of nails and began reading with his fingers what was left. He had erased almost everything. What remained is what is contained here. What remained is what was composed when there was almost nothing left— only a few letters, a phrase, a response to a question that no one claimed responsibility for asking. This second prisoner was offered freedom. He rejected this freedom of his captors, their freedom that depended upon eradication, upon the erasure of another's effort and resistance. In the place of their freedom he accepted imprisonment with another's poems, with another's desperation. He rejected the validity of the world insisted upon by his tormentors, the validity of inhumanity. Instead he submitted to something which had demonstrated itself, something which persisted in the very place where many labored to deny it: the humane.

~

To chew this
bread
with writing teeth

— Paul Celan

i followed the
no one, the
not now, the
no more...

a life-wide throat
welcomed me into
its oath—

(a final stone
thrown towards a freedom
fails and descends
and that distance is for me)

this silence.

~

i wait
        and a nether-written contract is drafted.
        silence winces and
i wait
        as cloth words its thread towards
        the moth-while
        madness fondles what the hand cannot find or
        still
i wait
        and this is all that is needed to condemn
        the home that calls each moment
        its shelter.

~

the no-ache
of the no-wide
no-moment writes itself into
heart-folds and child-soft
i-walls;

the thread of its no-code
(its no-trace) is
the self-salt of thirst
i follow.

~

what was cited
in this time-scratch-
welcome-
cement

whose initials
whose heart
whose arrow

~

whose effacement
left this nail to
lead this hand, letter-lost and sorrow-
thin across a floor of word-
less artifice?

~

here and not here

their sentence-
cradles

what-remains

        after-
words

                        ~

desire-wide and
wish-white—

        the cloth of all confinement
elicits dreams of
scissors;

                        ~

here
time is a witness

and i lower freedom's thread
into another's world
where time is
shadow.

                        ~

stolen or
lost:

the leash of ease
a lathe of modest sadnesses
false dearth
a tear trowel

the delicate root of a deferred self
a crown of want and correction
one heart-cane
rinds of nearness

the infections and treatments
and the half-lit
corridors of home.

~

time:
        calendrical
        hide and seed

        rift attired
        lettered metric

        home-wide
        self-chasmic
        loss-mortarred

        denial-sated
        emetic

        clot-wise
        mendicant

        now-encircled
        incidence

time:
        wordless
        consonant
        whole.

~

i came from

a seminal-chime in a thorn
-anointed and lord-wearied horde

threaded into the well-intentioned middle-twine

fecal and artless in dream and in effort

hardened on a diet of immolation and
slender contentment

i
fled into this
hide of riddle and fear.

~

led to this
no-lit
end-room

the world diminished to its elemental
claim:

a nail
flesh-warm
time scratched white into concrete
want

in charnel silence—

a reason to remain.

~

in fact—

the rose of ascent-
worn
effort,

here
the throne-cast
seed their descent
in a self-wild
manor.

for-
(now)-
wards

this hell /
weal-lesson.

in fact

the rows of assent
warn
effort.

hear
the thrown-caste
cede their dissent
in a self-wiled
manner—

fore-
(now)-
words

this hell
we'll lessen

~

death is one line
in the literate hand of the one who offers
direction
to a life that has
tread-word after tread-word
worn smooth all trace of intention.

Dialogues

Dialogues with Absence / Build Those Cages in Awe

Anagrams are re-letterings, re-wordings. The urge to create anagrams arises from an experience of otherness. It has been said that an anagram is a gesture of defiance, that it undoes something; It is also said to be redemptive as it builds something from what has been undone. An anagram demonstrates that whatever can be thought, spoken, written, can always be otherwise. The effort required to reveal, to speak with, this otherness indicates the considerable resistance towards such a *conversation*.

Everything is always speaking to what it is not.

Listen : Silent

Hans Bellmer; *The Anatomy of the Image*

truces
daily encoded in
denial;

a machine-lust rattles,
rhymes of sorrow,
a virulent hush,
and vainly discrete abuses lean...

and we want this

And I want to reveal scandalously the interior
that will always remain hidden and sensed
behind successive layers of human structure

31

Jacob Frank, *Sayings of the Lord*: **no.2043**

to thank the moment...

a wish,
a wound—
that the lover utters.

...and the heart must not reveal
what it knows to the mouth.

Genesis 1:1

the death-bearing hand
etching heaven
to engender it.

in the beginning
God created the heaven
and the earth.

Heidegger; *What is Metaphysics* **(The Answer to the Question)**

rations in an open hand
:
the song of despair.

                                        [as] dread is not an apprehension
                                                         of nothing.

Jalaluddin Rumi; *Mathnwi-i ma'nawi* **3:558**

a weary, joyless ground

the veiled whore of untruth
awaits
you:
    the quarried-word.

he who travels without a guide
requires two hundred years
for a two day journey.

Paul Celan; *Der Meridian*

a fen of duty

dream-ladders, saddened
stand rooted as gallows

no-mooring

                                              man's words groaned
                                          under an age-old load
                                     of false and distorted sincerity

Nelson Goodman; *Worlds and Worldmaking*

a pyre,
a mirror,

built in the lair of
reality

as little
wicked animals

age.

                                        reality in a world, like realism in a picture,
                                                  is largely a matter of habit.

GATT

derangement and terror
in a regal feast

General Agreement on Tariffs and Trade

Unica Zurn; *The House of Illnesses*

death mends
the day-web
fondly

i feed it
my honest
questions.

                                   the quietness of death yawned
                                   in the middle of my body's nest

Gregory M. Matoesian; *Reproducing Rape: Domination through Talk in the Courtroom*

the / our
uttered moment
winces

its enemy's stubborn voice,
without beauty,
becomes death's
ideal:

a criminal
ink-dance of
memory.

[his /] our communication succeeds
because we work, moment by moment,
to identify and remedy
the inevitable troubles that arise.

Roy A. Sorenson; *Thought Experiments*

the poet questions
        the anthem,
        the crib-dream,
        the sacred
milk of home.

certainties marching:
armour, eyes—
        i see
their itching

i sob.

                        there may be merit in making hard choices
                                but there is also merit in
                                questioning the premises
                        that seem to force the hard choice.

Walter Benjamin; *Theses on the History of Philosophy*

this barbaric, chaotic
machine-
moment...

    (frozen, i
    wait outside)

No!
i shout
if
love made mittens...

        There is no document of civilization
        which is not at the same time
        a document of barbarism.

Intrusions

token

here the streets are unmarried
leaf-strewn, tree-silent
moments of
expectation:
            penny-brown and palm-warm
november-kindled
tokens of loneliness—

we exchange them for mouthfuls
of winter's
dissent.

the word

from a distance
a passenger train is
language
overcoming the trauma of distance
rationally
a statement spoken across the landscape
each car is
a word
linked into a meaning
that remains constant
from its place of origin
to its destination.

~

but there is a door in every word
which opens
into the laughter and the coughing
the games and the sleep
the anxiety the tears and the whispers
the homecoming of
meaning–
        the unique endurance of distance
in the presence of others.

stone-song

the stone of me
the burden
you labored with
into the patience of your innermost chamber

where the chisel and the hammer
of each day, the sweep
and the brush of evening
rescued form from formlessness

the body the face the mouth
you blessed me
                    my voice–
the song of the stone that has emerged
will always sound

the gift
of your heart-worn hands.

respiration

death respires—
        armoured
triangulations of desire
(the withheld
tomorrow-lodged
in this other-lettered,
other-addressed
other[~~apart~~]ment)

death respires
mediation
distance
and pursuit.

the gift

un-gifts miscarried
from shore-body to shore-body

i mistook
the yearning—
ribbonned and knotted
lack,
the intention-wrapped
lack   that i

that i
lived
into the binding lie
that even the withheld was:
a thing to be received,
a thing to be undone and
possessed.

how did love come to you

along an intimate path of forgetting
with moss-covered knees
a flower in its wishing-throat
an accumulation of excuses for the infirm, grey-fingered future
laboring for each breath
nursing a litter of words
unbuttoned and clinging to a fence
the fright of winter drifting on the eye's horizon

how did love come to you

through a tear in the fabric of your blindness
with a promise protruding from its stem
in the morning of every caress
retreating, heartward and worldless
a stain of belonging
on the lip of an effort
asleep in the arms of its silence

how did love come to you.

disfigurement

disfigurements of loneliness
reside in performance—

upon the distraction of ill-conceived walls
abbreviations of desire
                (the memory of what has been
        half-lived)
in night-chalk
is hand-spoken.

machine

when something is forgotten:
a machine is left behind
as evidence; it coughs up the unlearned

we inhale— ash-words: in our lungs unspelled,
                     in our throats unpronounced,
                     on our tongues the unspeakable
polluting;

we open our mouths
and the drone of relentless activity
speaks over us

conversation becomes a submission
to the mechanical,
to what labors to exclude the uncontainable,

the unbound, the whispered
i love you—
            corroding tears
wept into the heartlessness
of every device—

               memory.

necropolitan

the necropolitan swirling
leaves
scratching something into the abandoned night-
street:

> *fathers do not die; they are assassinated*
> *mothers never die; they are stolen*
> *brothers, sisters do not die; they are hiding*
> *lovers cannot die; within the heart that is their home*
> *they endure*
> *the drifting*
> *blankets of effacement.*

intrusion

i begin to end
at the not-yet bridged,
the self-rift,
the thread-
wide intrusion of the world.

i retrace the almost-circles,
the re-birth and re-failure, the
i have done and i will do, or say think deny...
                    not-
rings of understanding
worn.

                                                  i begin
                                                 to end.

perspective

eyes raised from
local-words
to the end-spoken
personal horizon —

a self-declared abyss narrows into
the non-
specific grin of the landscape.

a frustrated landscape

a frustrated landscape
settled:

dwellings on either side of
a well-travelled narrow lie of names;

home, viscerally pronounced is
buttressed by emotional arch(e/i)te(x/c)ture;

in the background,
unspoken and understood, a river
and its reflective promise
all is not yet lost.

bed

clothed in october-light
i asked only for you
to kneel with me in the failed
garden of our common effort

let the weeds ring our fingers
let the cold earth still us
before an audience of leaves who have lost their green applause
let us look down from where we have climbed
and fall
i asked
only you
into love's autumn bed.

dearth

in a maze of night-
speech

the weight of a single hand
reaching into forgetfulness
is enough to sever
the black thread of yearning;

from the thread-rift
silence spills
and hardens into
uttered barriers.

love erases its name

Love erases its name: it
writes itself to you).
—Paul Celan

i am the sentence
love serves

in the illegible yard of a family's
un-doings

uttered into predictability
its routine haunts
the stone-bloom of a child's
chalk-drawn flower.

~

from the wall that has always been my limit
i watch

love
in its uniform of sacrifice

erases its name
because it does not recognize itself
in words.

palms

lovers practice
the tongue-stone
turning of breath
in the closed-hand
evening
park of my frequents walks;

they are not beacons
or ruins of my unlived
selves

their heart-measured suffering
does not follow
the cadence of my deliberate
(step)thinking—

      no, i am
i am
only the flesh-uttered
fear
that moistens their palms.

the passage

you forget
you order words
into the passage
where the other that is your insufficiency
always appears

clothed in your orphan-words
it is this other
for which a love declares itself
and with which a love occupies itself;

but, it is only after this other unfastens
your words,
it can only be
once
the hidden skin of incomprehensibility
presents itself
that your love can rise
speechless and
truth-erect.

the anomaly

tacit leash—
        the anomaly is restrained
by expectation

i see a net and not what struggles
to free itself

i call the net *home*:
an inheritance of tears and the unspoken
knotted into hallucinations that (pre/dis)figure

the word-faced-moments
the reaching

hands
years

      i cast
    i cast
i cast a net
and rid myself
of consequence and effort.

Shelter

A first sign of the beginning of understanding is the wish to die. This life seems unbearable, another unattainable. One is no longer ashamed of wanting to die; one begs to be moved out of the old cell, which one hates, into a new one which one must first learn to hate. One is also moved by a certain residual faith that, during transport, the master will happen to come along the corridor, look at the prisoner and say: 'This man is not to be locked up again. He comes to me."

— Franz Kafka

And yet perhaps this is the reason you cry,
this is the nightmare you wake screaming from:
being forever
in the pre-trembling of a house that falls

— Galway Kinnel,
The Book of Nightmares

the neighbourhood has been destroyed, my house has been destroyed. only a portion of a wall remains standing. there is a painting hanging on this wall. it is an abstraction: a black outline of a circle, imperfect, broken, shaded red inside at its bottom; the circle is imposed on a green background, the green is the colour of leaves when the sun shines through them. scattered along this green landscape are lines and polygons, barely visible as though sediments, fossils.

this painting was not painted by a child.

it is the only thing of its kind.

it is the reason everything everywhere is being destroyed. the destruction is afraid of this image, of this work, and so everything must be eradicated so that nothing will remain for the painting to appeal to, so that no one will remain for this image, for this work, to shelter.

~

understanding is
the bleeding
of concrete and skin—
their unnameable mingling,
puddled-
truth.

~

to flee the understanding
others have
raised

     the home
where thinking has no door to close behind itself,
where the roof collapses upon every attempt
to speak
     the ruin
where living is:

a nail
where nothing has been hung
for as long as anyone can
remember,

an inability to separate
our tears from our soup,
inherited,

(from mouth to hand to mouth)
a tired passing of persistence
around a table where the crumbs of past gatherings
are never wiped away.

~

the unmeasured and unsound
heaven has been approximated
above us

our dreaming flakes
from a sagging ceiling

walls drunk with winter
re-tell the only holes they know

a blanket is pulled over us
for comfort
        the dead are comfortable
and to keep us from reaching
        they do not wake in the night's heart
for something that others have failed
        screaming in the arms of silence
to grasp.

~

certainty is a parade
language suffers
in its streets

~

meaning
streams from the eyes,
coalesces in the half-filled
sentence

~

the family the primeval forest
the shelter

where the ground is a punishing father,
a muddy path never mistaken

where leaves are warnings
a mother hangs
over her children:

> *the rain despises the cowering we are born into;*
> *the wind rewards only the disheveled;*
> *a thunderstorm is a rumour of infidelity;*
> *please pray the snow does not*
> *come, it will lead you into forgetting...*

the reiterated erection
of an idea that was never meant to be
lived in

the family the primeval
shelter

where some things, miscarried
peek from within words that have been
split
and not broken.

~

the mouths of the first speakers
open
she-dark
wings in a sky of not-yet
words—

obedient dwellings
infested
with humanity

with humanity

the original word is
not alone in its darkness.

~

born
into the shelter of hands
we have already outgrown
the walls split into fingers
unable to contain our screaming
and our squirming—
the first syllables
of an attempt we have evolved into
accepting.

~

delivered
into the slap of misapprehension
silenced and spoken for
a pre-determined name already set loose
into the winter of our future
its dark prints and its urine
marking every moment.

~

held briefly
in arms where the moist and trembling quiet of memory
comes unbound from the throb of what cannot live
in the space of a single life—

into an absence that is love,
we are lifted
away from the remembering-skin
away from the milk of understanding.

~

tears in the bread that will not rise
hunger unadorned
fumbling with the key and the lock

~

the hole-speaking
within
a shallow pocket :

the mouth of every
question is
its answer

~

resistance—
that *pestilence* of dignity
is a child's distaste
for the stone in its throat
for the stone in every throat
for the stone that no one could fathom
                              could be
shifted by breathing the world in
                              could be
hauled up to the tongue by the breath's turning
                              could be
spit
into the unblinking
eyes of habit.

~

self-elaborated
home of memory—
in rooms of dream and thought
our hands are always
as filthy as the walls,
as the floor

the soot of privilege
exhaled inhaled
black apple, black bread
we swallow, unseeing
the stain of bitterness that everything is
forced into wearing

                              the uniformity, the mineral

darkening
leaching
heartward.

~

a temple is a shelter,
a misapprehension of permanence

shelter is a permanent
response to the unspeakable

permanence is the unspeakable
temple of suffering.

~

the eye staring outward
through a hole in wall of the *common good*
sickened by the unhealing
wounds of *necessity* ;

the finger poking inward
through a hole in the wall of the *common good*
never touching the affluent
ridicule of *sacrifice* .

~

"where there is no sign there is no ideology"
(from Langer; *Philosophy in a New Key*)

where there is no ideology
there is no child
waving to a passing plane

~

the rake of duty
draws the fallen leaves of everyone
towards the autumn-pile of being

~

in my grandfather's boots i
stumble down cellar steps

i bleed into the sleeve of the jacket my mother wore
after slicing a lip on the cracked rim of a bottle
after capitulating to the paternal clock that has wound its way
through generations, leading them all
to ruin
without flinching.

~

i blow the dust from a book
no one ever reads
because it is the dust we value

i cough and it is someone else's penny
directed towards a debt i pay for
by breathing,
by insisting

all that has been buried
can be unearthed, can be used once more
and then re-buried

all insignificance
hidden away in boxes, in envelopes
even the most insignificant
is a fist-sized stone when re-discovered,

when raised and thrown...

a pane of glass
        where the past once breathed persists
        as a bubble, trapped
        as an imperfection, living
is the margin of home.

~

a foundation is laid as a riddle for living to solve

that is the underbelly of every dwelling,
the male-ferment:
the rage, thick-fingered and literal,
the dank refusal to emerge from
the belief that answers lie
in the violent openings of maternal barrels.

~

how to stand beneath the collapsing seasons

~

> *a nail can be held*
> *and a nail can hold*
>   *a body,*
> *suspended*

> *to understand is the struggle*
> *not to know*

~

a possession is evidence that we have followed
a loneliness which has run far ahead of us

loss
this is the path our futility imagines
loneliness has taken.

~

unmoving, unbreathing
knowledge is raised to awe,
to convince—

a memorial:

every thing has its proper place;
error is disorder,
disturbance.

~

the chant of understanding
permeates
the cracks in the walls of knowledge, encourages
collapse:

all things
inflect
to be;
they need
no rest
they name
no place
their home.

~

the ideal of order, of the unmoving
unmovable

bullied into extreme postures
and tortured with occupancy—

building despises its materials

because it dreads them:

because when a brick is held to the ear
one can hear the crumbling
of everything that has ever been
created in the image of permanence.

~

trance-words
shuffled into memory
's hand

~

assurance keeps us all
waiting

in its absence,

trembling, we
are the excluded
middle

~

the follower wears a shoe of fear and a shoe of love:

a sole, worn-out,
admits
the pebble of dying.

we are never led into understanding
but only to a fence we are instructed to hold,
or a wall we are forced into facing;

there
we must not speak, or open our eyes, or move
or in any way disturb
the irrevocable
aim of genius.

~

to speak with you
every word turns its back
to everyone else
                    and petrifies
                    (and on such familiar hardness
                    we hang pictures,
                    their backs to the world)

the well intentioned utterance
is our peaceful sleep:

this/my house
is a door locking

this/my family
employs something unspeakable
to chase away the homeless who cling to
its property

this/my life
i want i mean i don't want
i am, or will be: these
are our privileged silences,
the darknesses which conceal
the sneaking and the searching and the fumbling
of those driven to break into us

~

breathing
the circle is born
dying
the circle persists
breathing
the circle is the world
for every other form:

      laughing-square
      weeping-line
      the terrified-
      dimensionless-
      singularity.

~

      estrangement
      still in its childhood
      circling
      pole-words

~

when the concealing collapses
and our predicament drips into our sleeping mouths

when there is nothing to console what is home-weary
in our thinking

we find ourselves handfirst
in fields seeded with truth-
rubble:

      we find ourselves
explaining how a stone and a nail
and a charred piece of wood
are the playing-pieces in a game
we find ourselves explaining, again and again,
to the uninhabited
human-space
                that is our burden.

~

understanding is the admission—

a rusted pail collecting
rainwater dripping through a crack in the bitter-wood
ceiling of a house which cringes alongside others,
speechless before the indifference
                            of tides.

~

masturbatory
thought
circles

~

day-lessened,
(intracellular transmissions of) learned
dying

~

the tent of illness:

the human supports
the sag of exhausted sky

   understood

we are all
lived into this ground where

   understanding

the sky's decaying fabric is
knotted around our unyielding.

~

the temporary imagined as permanent /
detour of experience

the unreachable, indefinitely deferred,
reduced to a predicament,
to an already-inhabited
name-taking
address.

repairs are undertaken,
locks (un-thought) replaced,
curtains (un-spoken) cleaned and re-hung.

the detour
is a journey walled
adequately but not completely
the sky, the unbearable overabundance,
abysmal in every crack—
                              its voice-
gusts:
        of experience

(*the lostness-seasoned*
shelter
assumed
to be
contentment).

~

a silence of ignorance
outweighs
a silence of recognition

~

(heart-blue-
prints of unknowing)

~

a child's room is built
in the basement of reason

where time develops
cracks as slight as an insect's effort
(which widen with acceptance
as well as with questioning)

until mornings are night-soaked
and presents are future-infested

and the door and its lock represent
the perfect union of indecision and
fear

      sorrow-transparent
voices support the indisputable
walls which were raised to keep the child
in.

~

      in the basement-
uncertainty the child develops
cracks as slight as the wound
of an insufficient language.

~

seeded
in memory
a mother-father-voice
gasping—
> *looking down at the ground we saw*
> *and we understood*
> *there was nothing*
> *to support us or to keep us*
> *in place*

i live because floors have been spoken
and thought
for my support,
surfaces of faith
verifiable and self-evident
streets and paths and fields and ...

  in winter
a pond freezes over and i
walk on water with knives
strapped to the soles of my boots.

~

bone-uttering

determinations of the skeletal

silence

~

snowfield: the other face
of the night sky

vigilance and

dread
in mute performance

currency

poetry, endlessly negotiated...

nothing is
ever-settled